SINISTER TENNIS

SINISTER TENNIS

HOW TO PLAY AGAINST AND WITH
LEFT-HANDERS

by Peter Schwed

UNITED STATES LAWN TENNIS ASSOCIATION

TENNIS INSTRUCTIONAL SERIES

Illustrations by George Janes

DOUBLEDAY & COMPANY, INC.
GARDEN CITY, NEW YORK
1975

This book is dedicated to
My favorite left-hander in the world,
my daughter Kathy,

and

My doubles partner for many years,
lefty Andy Rowan

and

A left-hander whose book I edited
and who was kind enough on a couple of
occasions to allow me on the court with him
and not make me look too silly, Rod Laver.

ISBN: 0-385-06706-2 Trade
0-385-06368-7 Paperbound
Library of Congress Catalog Card Number 73–20530

Contents

sin-is ter, adj. 1. of or on the left side (from the Latin *sinistra*).

2. threatening or portending evil, harm or trouble, ominous.

CHAPTER 1

Is This Book Necessary?

You are a right-handed tennis player.

What are the chances that you will run up against a left-handed opponent:

1) As a member of the crowd with whom you normally play?
2) Just wandering around and trying to pick up a game?
3) In a tournament?

And what are the odds in a doubles match that:

4) Your partner is a left-hander?
5) One of the opposing pair is?
6) That, in a tournament, you'll face at least one southpaw?

A generation or two ago, the whole idea of writing even a short complete book on the subject of playing tennis against, and with left-handers would have been absurd. There just weren't enough of them around to be worth worrying about, and writing a book specifically about problems and tactics involved in playing them would have been like taking out an insurance policy against being hit on the head by a falling safe. If a baby boy or girl showed a tendency to try to murder the breakfast Pablum with a spoon held in his or her left hand, Mother grabbed the spoon, thrust it into the infant's right hand, and kept the left one securely in her own.

So practically all the natural southpaws grew up to be converted right-handers. Ambitious athletically inclined fathers sometimes wondered wistfully if they'd made a mistake forcing Junior to play games right-handed, when they saw what an edge left-handers had in professional baseball, both as pitchers and as batters, but they reconciled themselves. Fame and money weren't everything. After all, everyone knew that left-handers were likely to be a little *crazy*. This was a tradition encouraged in baseball life by the eccentric Rube Marquard and in baseball literature by Ring Lardner.

Then, as mid-century approached, so did the Age of Psychoanalysis and along with it the understanding that the forcible changing of one's natural "handedness" was very likely to be damaging. The Pablum flew where it would, regardless of which hand was wielding the spoon. And the number of left-handers grew and flourished.

So today, how many left-handers are there? It is not a question that can be answered easily or with any statistical certainty. The census-takers don't ask it. But one out of six of the members of the Professional Bowlers Association, which numbers over one thousand top competitors, is left-handed, and this seems as good a sample as a public-opinion poll is likely to produce. If a bowler is born left-handed or right-handed he will probably have no urge to convert to the other side. There is a slight advantage in being left-handed if you're a top star on the tour (you don't bowl into the "groove" that is worn into alleys by countless right-handers), but it's a factor that is minor, and it isn't worth learning to use one's unnatural hand and arm. Similarly, although there actually is a substantial advantage to being a lefty tennis player, it is not so marked that I ever heard of anyone who tried to convert himself or herself to that style of play.

There are games where it's a real asset to be left-handed, notably baseball, where southpaw pitchers are needed and left-handed sluggers not only have a much shorter fence to clear but also start from the batter's box a good step nearer first base. Therefore a researcher would find that the proportion of left-handed big leaguers to right-handers would be considerably more than one in six. Baseball statistics in this respect would not offer a fair sample, however, since so many ball players see the advantage of converting and do so, if they're capable of it.

Golf is another game which can't be used as a valid sample of the right-handedness or left-handedness of athletes generally. It's a distinct disadvantage to play left-handed in golf, particularly in the matter of the golf equipment that's available and secondarily in the way golf course architecture is laid out. It's comparatively easy to learn to swing a golf club from the other side, just the way good baseball hitters pick up the art of becoming switch hitters, and I would suspect this happens frequently if a natural left-handed person has real golfing ambitions. The statistics about the proportion of left-handed golf professionals would unquestionably show that the ratio of left-handers to right-handers would be far less than one in six. Bob Charles, the great New Zealand pro, is the only top-notcher who springs immediately to mind as being left-handed.

So neither baseball nor golf samples are representative of the ordinary person's likelihood of being left-handed, but there doesn't seem to be any reason why bowling statistics would not be. I believe the one-in-six ratio is a realistic figure, and casual observation also confirms it pretty well, so it is the figure I'll use in answering the questions posed at the outset of this chapter.

1) If you normally play with about half a dozen friends, one of them is likely to be a left-hander.

2) Once in six times a casual pick-up opponent is likely to be one.

3) In the course of a tournament, with a draw of thirty-two contestants, if you go to the finals you will play five rounds. It's a little worse than even money that you'll run up against a southpaw. If there are sixty-four in the draw, it *is* even money.

4) The odds that you are partnered in doubles with a left-hander are five-to-one against. In other words, not probable but not at all impossible.

5) The odds that one of your opponents in a doubles match will be a southpaw drop sharply, since there are two chances for one of them to be one. The chances are now only two and a half to one against.

6) In a thirty-two-draw doubles tournament, where you go to the finals, you're likely to encounter a southpaw. The odds are five-to-three in favor of it. In a sixty-four-draw tournament, the chances are two-to-one in favor of it.

Confirmation of the emergence of a tremendously greater number of left-handed players in the world of tennis in recent years can readily be seen just inspecting the rosters of the great. Prior to this century, the top southpaw was Bob Wrenn, winner of the U. S. Singles title four times in the 1890s. Since 1900, in men's cham-

Bob Wrenn.

John Doeg.

pionship tennis, there were only four outstanding male left-handers before 1950. Beals C. Wright won our National Championship in 1905 and was ranked in the first ten every year throughout the first decade of the century. The great Australian, Sir Norman E. Brookes, put that nation on top in 1909, 1910, 1911, and again in 1914. R. Lindley Murray beat Bill Tilden to win our Championship in 1918, two years before Tilden began his long dominance of the game. John Doeg won in 1930.

That ends it. Of course there were unquestionably other outstanding left-handers around then, notably Carl Earn and Seymour Greenberg in this country, but none of them seem to have been good enough to inscribe his name in the record books at top National Championship levels.

Now take a look at what left-handed tennis players have achieved since 1950, and how many there are around today in top-flight competition. Art Larsen took Forest Hills in 1950. Jaroslav Drobny came through to win Wimbledon in 1954. Neale Fraser took the United States Championship in 1959 and again in 1960, in which year he also won the Wimbledon crown. And, of course, the classic left-hander since Norman Brookes, Rod Laver, not only achieved the Grand Slam of tennis, the winning of all four major championships in one year, twice—in 1962 and in 1969—but also tacked on a couple of other Wimbledon singles titles in 1961 and 1968.

Also in the top level during the modern era have been, and still are, Mervyn Rose, Owen Davidson, Tony Roche, Roger Taylor, Nicki Pilic, Joaquin Loyo-Mayo, Mark Cox, Torben Ulrich, Jim McManus, Roscoe Tanner, Jan Leschley, Ivan Molina, Manuel Orantes, El Shafei, John Paish,

Rod Laver.

Jimmy Connors.

Ray Ruffels, Guillermo Vilas, and Jimmy Connors. I'm sure I've overlooked many others, to whom I apologize.

There don't seem to have been so many left-handed women players, either in the old days or now. I don't know why unless mothers have been more solicitous about their baby girls developing Rube Marquard tendencies. In any case, there has been a great scarcity of top-notch left-handers among the ladies, two very notable exceptions being Kay Stammers, some years back, and Ann Haydon Jones, more recently, both of England. Kristy Pigeon is an outstanding young American woman player who is left-handed and there are two foreign girls, each only in her middle-to-late teens, who are both lefties and who promise to rate among the best in the world in the years to come. They are Dianne Fromholtz, of Australia, and Martina Navratilova, of Czechoslovakia.

Beverly Baker Fleitz, one of the most enchanting players to watch when she was in her tennis prime in the years just after World War II, belongs in the list of left-handers because she was truly ambidextrous. She was not like great two-handed players of certain shots, such as Pancho Segura, Chris Evert, Cliff Drysdale, and Peaches Bartkowicz: they are essentially right-handers who use two hands on frequent occasions as an aid to strength or control. Mrs. Fleitz, on the other hand, *never hit a backhand* shot. She switched her racket from one hand to the other as she saw to which side the ball was coming and then belted a powerful forehand regardless of which hand she was using. There never was anyone else quite like her, and she could truly be called "half left-handed." The nearest thing to her today is the South African

John Bromwich.

Frew McMillan, who uses the two-hand technique off both wings.

One other two-handed old-time star had a technique more like Segura and Evert and Company, in that he used both hands for certain shots, but he belongs in this southpaw list more than they or than Mrs. Fleitz or McMillan, because he was essentially left-handed. This great player, surely one of the finest doubles performers in history, was the Australian John Bromwich. If a ball came to his left hand side he hit it conventionally, using a left-hand forehand, and he served lefty. But if he was taking the ball to his right, he employed both hands on that side.

This essentially means that Bromwich was a true left-hander, who merely got more power into his backhand by bringing the other hand into play. If you were on a court with Bromwich you were facing or partnered with a southpaw. This is not the case if you're playing with Segura, Drysdale, Evert, or Bartkowicz.

All of this is, of course, background, and its intention is just to explain that no tennis player who takes the game seriously can overlook what was once mere possibility but is now a quite likely probability. Today you will encounter left-handers often enough that the very special knowledge and attitude you need is as important as all the other unusual but vital things a good tennis player equips himself to meet, such as varying court surfaces and conditions, weather, and freak shots.

CHAPTER 2

The Left-hander
as Singles Opponent

A WINNING TIP

The first thing a pair of singles rivals do before a match, after shaking hands, is to spin a racket to determine who serves and who gets choice of court. In most matches, serving first is enough of an advantage that the winner of the toss invariably indicates that he will serve and leaves the comparatively unimportant matter of court selection to his opponent.

When you are going to play a left-hander, however, a factor may well exist which you can use profitably. During the summer months within a couple of hours on either side of noon, it's likely that each of you will have the problem of playing into the sun when you're on the wrong side of the net. So flip the racket, and whether you win or lose take a thoughtful look at the sun's position.

If you have won the toss, and are a particularly strong server, you will probably elect to serve first and take your chances about your lefty opponent's figuring out the edge he may now be able to obtain by being as smart as you would have been had you chosen court. But if you are not a particularly powerful server, or if you lose the toss of the racket, by all means start out on the court that's going to give you an edge over the first two games. You may well break your opponent's serve right away and be able to run out the set as a result.

The most troublesome thing about playing into the sun comes on one's service, when the ball has to be thrown up so high that the player is blinded. No eyeshade or peaked cap has ever been able to combat this problem effectively, nor are even the best sunglasses a solution because, once the ball is in play, you just don't see it as well through dark glasses. So serving into the sun is often a horror that can disturb the finest of players and actually destroy a lesser performer.

Let's look at the various possibilities with respect to the flip of the racket:

1) You have won the toss and elect to serve because, sun or not, you have confidence in your serve. Fair enough, and this special tip does not apply because either your opponent will be cagey enough to make the sun work for *him* in choosing court or he won't, in which case everything has just been handed to you on a platter.

2) You have won the toss but you have no substantial confidence that having first serve gives you any particular advantage. In that case, instead of choosing to serve, select your court so that *he* will have to start the first game serving into the sun. Opponents change courts after the first game and so, when you start serving the second game, you won't be serving squarely into the sun as he had to (even though facing in its direction) because you are right-handed while he is left-handed. Your toss will be to the other side of the body than his is. If he tries to outsmart you by electing to receive (which is his privilege but one he's unlikely to adopt), you're still in good shape. Now

you serve first from the shady court, and he will serve the second game from there. The first time you'll have to serve into the sun will be on the third game. It's just as if you had won both serve *and* choice of courts on the toss.

3) You have lost the toss. Here the strategy is the same as in (2) above. If your opponent chooses to serve first, as is likely, make sure he has to serve into the sun. If he chooses court, which is unlikely, you can either serve or elect to receive, if sun conditions appear more important to you than serving first.

Admittedly there will be a large part of the day when sun conditions are such, that all this cleverness can't be used. The sun won't be in either of your eyes no matter from where you're serving. In that case, just hope to win the toss and serve first. But there will be many times when this "winning tip" can be employed so don't overlook it when the sun is high in the heavens.

All of this advice is academic, of course, if your game is indoors or under a bubble or staged in winter in the Arctic Circle.

Your Handicap

The first thing to implant firmly in your mind when you find yourself facing a left-handed rival of comparable skills to your own is that you start with a very considerable handicap. Each of you has, as a rule, been playing against right-handed players, and you are just another one as far as he is concerned. He doesn't have to vary his normal game in any respect at all. If he were up against *another* left-hander he'd have the same problems you're going to face. But he isn't: you are right-handed and everything he knows or is capable of using on a tennis court can be brought to bear to beat you.

What about everything *you* know or are capable of using? Obviously whatever good attributes you own in your tennis game are not just going to melt away but *everything* that usually makes you a winner is going to be handled inversely. All of the mechanics of your game, both on the offense and the defense, will require adjustment, but if you are a sound player you can probably cope after a few minutes with things such as unusual variations in the spin of the ball, which is the biggest edge the left-hander has on you. The thing that is hard to maintain is unflagging concentration on the fact that you are facing a southpaw, and all of your natural and patterned reflexes that have been grooved into your strokes and strategy have to be reversed. It's a little like when a man borrows his wife's raincoat, or she his. Reach instinctively to button or unbutton it and you're on the wrong side.

Concentration

Concentration is almost the first thing that a tennis instructor emphasizes to a beginner, and it is certainly true that the ability to shrug off the last point and bear down wholeheartedly on the next is often the difference between a winning performance and a losing one. On the whole, however, tennis concentration has to do with not letting your mind wander away from what you have to do right now: keeping one's eye on the ball; getting one's feet into position for the shot; getting the racket head back in early preparation; deciding upon the shot you're going to make and its direction. After a while, a good player will learn to concentrate instinctively, and will carry through with sound technique most of the time.

There will be occasions when he goes astray for one reason or the other and realizes that he is taking his eye off the ball or is failing to turn his side to the net sufficiently on certain shots, but he will then consciously concentrate on rectifying such a lapse and will correct them within a few points. For this reason even a first-rate player, whose stroke production is beautifully grooved into a pattern of play, can never let his mind drift off into thoughts of the evening that lies ahead or what happened at the office yesterday. It's hard to maintain unflagging concentration throughout a match, from first point to last, but every great player or coach will tell you that it is very possibly the most important single winning trait a tennis player can cultivate.

Concentration takes on much greater importance for a right-hander when he meets a southpaw opponent, and that is a blatant understatement. Its importance becomes almost immeasurable. Unless you *constantly* are aware that your rival is left-handed, with full appreciation of how that affects both his and your own strokes and battle plan, you are going to lose, presuming you're evenly matched in talent.

So the added burden of having to concentrate at every moment of a match upon things that are no part of your ingrained habits of play is the biggest hurdle you have to surmount in taking on a left-hander. All of the information or advice that follows in this chapter could be understood and followed by you if they applied to a one-time or infrequent situation which you could see coming up. That isn't the case. When you're up against a left-hander, you must have in the forefront of your mind "He's a lefty!" all through the match, and gear your strokes, defenses, and tactics to suit this particular situation. It will do you no good at all to know intellectually how to handle a left-hander unless you apply what you know throughout the whole contest. That takes concentration.

Every time you're crowded behind the baseline by your opponent's forcing shot and have to throw up a high defensive lob in order to give yourself a chance to survive and get back into position, experience and instinct would be likely to try to direct it off to the right of center. Against anyone except a left-hander, that's the thing to do. If you haven't succeeded in lobbing well and deep, at least he may have to put the ball away with a backhand overhead smash, and not many people do that well. Or if you've pulled off a really effective, deep lob, the point may swing to where he now is forced into a defensive return off his backhand.

It all makes sense and everything in your normal pattern of play and instinctive reaction would see to it that you lobbed that way. But *no!* This guy is a lefty! Try to toss this lob up to the *other* corner—the one to which you seldom lob! Maybe you can and will do it as well as if you were making the other directional shot but there's no denying the fact that you have two things going against you. It doesn't fit your physical "groove," and you have to *remember* each time that it's the percentage shot. That takes concentration, and this circumstance is only an example of the whole variety of different ploys that you have to bear in mind on every point when you face a left-handed rival. Every stratagem has to be reversed in mirror fashion.

The tennis player who loses matches he should win because he can't maintain his focus of attention throughout the play will certainly be a dead duck when he's up against a left-hander of equal merit. Concentration is a must for any serious player, but when you're hard-pressed by a southpaw the necessity for maintaining it is doubled.

Serving

When you yourself are serving against a lefty, your problems are very little more than under normal conditions. This is the easiest portion of the revised game to which you have to adapt. You are not on the run and don't have to react to a ball that's coming at you. You can approach the service line leisurely, think what you want to do, and then do it. In this case all you have to bear in mind is to do the opposite of what you might normally plan to do, but since you have all the time in the world to contemplate that before you execute it, there's nothing particularly hard about carrying it out. It's true that mechanically your service will probably vary a bit, but not enough to be harmful unless you allow yourself to become neurotic about it. If, for example, you are trying to exploit your rival's weakness on a backhand return, against a right-hander, when serving from the deuce (or right-hand) court, you would stand very near the center of the service line and serve down the center. Serving from the ad (or left-hand) court, you would move much farther toward the corner and serve wide. Against a left-hander you'd have to do the opposite, but of all the difficulties involved in such a match, this one is the least.

Your slice serve, the easiest, safest, and least-tiring of all good service actions, is one you should normally rely upon a great deal in any match. Against a left-hander, it's even more effective than against the stream of right-handers you usually encounter, for your slice slides off to your left, or to his right which is, of course, his backhand. So stick with the slice serve even more than usual and try to accentuate its spin. This is one of the few aspects of facing a lefty where playing your normal stroke actually works out better than if you were up against a righty.

Receiving Serve

Conversely, receiving a good left-hander's service is likely to be the most difficult aspect you have to face in such a game. It's true that, as opposed to having to take the ball on the run, you can set yourself into position when you're the service receiver and you may even very

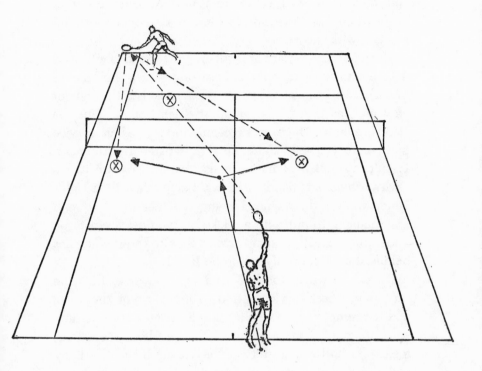

A slice serve is effective against a left-hander. (So is his slice against you, a right-hander, as you can see if you hold this drawing up to a mirror.)

well know exactly what sort of serve is coming up. Those advantages may not help you very much at the moment of truth, for left-handers are traditionally strong servers and their deliveries come at you both from different angles than you're accustomed to see and, even more important, with the reverse spin.

Mechanically I cannot explain why good southpaws do seem to have exceptionally strong serves. Rod Laver says that they make more use of their wrists throughout play and, as a result, develop stronger wrists. This, he claims, enables them to slice and top-spin their service balls more viciously than the rigid-wristed right-hander. I can't say that explanation makes complete sense to me —why *should* left-handers be wristier players than right-handers?—but there's no denying the fact that the spin they manage to put onto a wicked serve does seem to be something special, and if anyone should know what lies behind it all it certainly would be Rod Laver.

It's equally true for left-handers, of course, that the slice is the best service action to use most of the time, and it is employed in quality tennis on an overwhelming percentage of service points. On the slice, the server tosses the ball a little forward and away from the body and the racket is swung around it with contact being made on what can be visualized as the ball's outer and upper "corner." As explained before, when a right-hander serves a slice, this produces a sliced spin, which reverses itself upon hitting the court and slides off to the server's left, or to a right-handed receiver's forehand. Obviously the exact opposite happens when a left-hander pounds his slice into a right-handed receiver's service box. The ball bites fiercely off to the right-handers *backhand*. So the southpaw gets the same advantage in serving a slice to you that you do to him. Each of you, when receiving a slice serve, will find the bounce and spin unfamiliar and what is more it's coming in on the backhand side.

Facing a left-hander's wicked slice serve in the right-hand or deuce box is bad enough, but it doesn't draw you out of court. Even if the ball comes right into your body or off to your backhand after the bounce, you can at least punch or block it back and maintain court position. But when a lefty winds up on the left or ad side and whips a slice to your backhand, you often not only have to scramble past the sideline but, even if you make a good backhand return from there, you may well have to catch an express bus to get back near center court in time to get near your opponent's next shot. So concentrate on winning that point in the deuce court because the cards are stacked against you when you move over to the left court.

A lefty's flat serve coming at you isn't that different from a right-hander's and poses comparatively minor problems. The slight deviation in the angle of the on-coming ball, occasioned by his hitting it perhaps a couple of feet farther to his left (your right) than you are accustomed to see, doesn't matter enough to deserve anything more than this mention. What a lefty can achieve most effectively on occasions with a hard flat serve is when he's serving to you in the ad court. After a series of previous points when he has had you climbing into the side grandstand trying to return his slice, you are mentally set to expect to have to go toward the outside line and may even have taken up your receiver position a bit more that way than usual. That may be the moment when

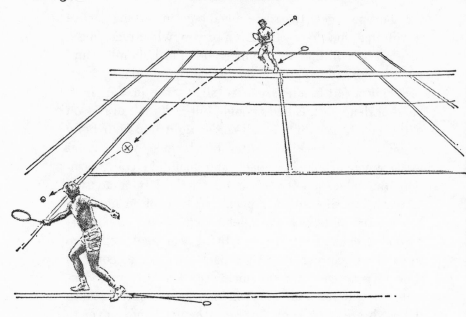

Lefty's slice serve coming at you in the advantage box.

your sinister opponent bangs a fast, flat serve right into
the deep center corner of your service box for a clean ace
past your forehand.

The twist, or reverse top-spin serve, also known as a
"kicker," is a most effective one to have in your armory
of weapons, assuming you're physically up to employing
it. Most weekend players are not. It imposes an unnatural
strain both on the back and the elbow, requires considerable strength and wrist snap, and for most tennis players
produces more lower back disc trouble and cases of tennis
elbow than it does winning points. Its virtue, if you're
capable of serving that way, is that it's a very sure serve

to go into your opponent's service box safely, since it clears the net comfortably high but its top spin makes it dip quickly and not travel too deep. Then it takes a very high, nasty bounce to your rival's backhand (if you're playing a right-hander). This usually makes it a marvelous serve against right-handers, particularly in doubles. But if a left-hander uses a twist against you, a right-hander, the bounce is going to come up high to your forehand and comparatively slowly. If you like to take a ball on the rise, anywhere from waist-to-chest high, you can step in and murder that serve. I've often found that left-handers don't realize this, keep on using the twist for their second serves, and wonder why it isn't producing very good results for them. Playing a good right-hander, if I were a lefty I'd forget my twist serve most of the time and stick to the slice. If you come up against a southpaw who doesn't do that, take advantage of it! You may break his service more often than you hold your own.

When you are serving against a good lefty, he'll have the same potential advantage if you give him a kicker, so tuck your twist away generally for that match and save it for the next right-hander you meet.

More About Returning a Lefty's Service

The slice serve comes wide to your forehand in the deuce court. If a right-hander had served it up, you would be likely to be able to play it stylishly. The ball slides away from you and, in taking your step or steps to reach it, you can turn your left side to the net in picture-book form, reach out to take the ball well away from your body, and execute whatever shot you think best under the circumstances.

But now it's a left-hander who slices his serve onto your forehand wing. The ball hits the court and then veers in toward your body. It cramps your shot so that you either have to open your stance or, if you're trying to get your side to the net, you have to pull your right leg back and step away from the oncoming ball. When you do that you lose the momentum of getting your body into the shot. So unless you're able to take the ball very early on the rise, before the full effect of the slice is evident, the best you are likely to be able to do is to block or punch the ball back without a full stroke. Since this is usually a fairly defensive shot, where would be the best percentage place toward which to direct it?

No firm rule can be promulgated about this any more than about any tennis tactic: variety is a prime asset in an effective game. On the whole, however, and against most left-handers who don't own Rod Laver's backhand, try to punch your shot cross-court. The lefty rushing the net against you has to take the ball low and mid-court on his backhand. That's not a situation where he's apt to be able to put the ball away, and that's about all you can expect to achieve when you've been forced to return serve un-aggressively.

Suppose you're still in the deuce court, but this time the slice serve has been directed to your backhand? Now it bounces *away* from your body but at least you are able to take a proper swing at it. Despite the fact that you are taking the ball near the center of the court, which normally from the standpoint of the geometric angles offers scantier open court toward which to hit passing shots, this is one circumstance where I feel you have very decent alternatives. Apart from the fact that you can

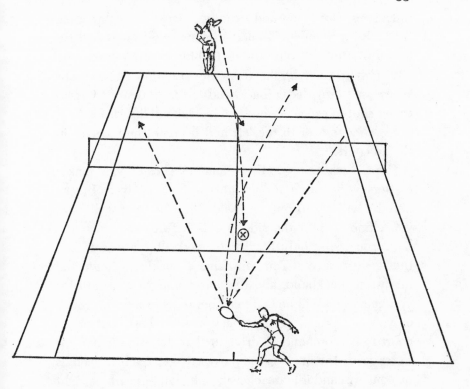

Lefty serves a slice down the center line in the deuce court.
(The mirror image of this drawing would show you doing the
same against a lefty from the ad court.)

make a more comfortable stroke, the same directional
shot to your opponent's backhand is open to you but now
you should be able to try anything from a backhand
drive to a dink. Just as important, the angle now exists
for a sharply angled backhand off to your right and out
of reach for your opponent, even if he's a scrambler. If
you can pull off such a shot effectively, he's got an aw-

fully long way to go and in an uncomfortable direction, if he's been following to net. Finally, you might well try to keep him nervous about rushing net by occasionally lobbing over his head in this situation. When your stroke isn't crowded, a backhand lob is in many ways an easier shot to execute well than a forehand lob is.

Let's move over to the left and become the receiver in the ad court.

Here is where a good left-hander's slice service makes matters very rough for a right-handed receiver. Invariably he will try to pull you wide, and he may well have you climbing into the side stands before you reach the ball. You really only have two good alternatives if he's that good a server. You can drive a backhand down the line to his backhand, and this has a margin of safety for you because it will be coming from outside into the court, or you can punch or slice back a low, short shot cross-court to his forehand. A drive in that direction is not apt to be good: the angle is too narrow to escape his reach as he comes in and if he reaches it, as he will, the whole right side of your court is open for his return. A low, short shot that he can't take above the height of the net, however, can be effective. He will have to hit it up and you have a chance to scurry back into position to take it.

In singles, a lob is not likely to be effective in this case either. Stroking from your extreme wide position, there is practically nowhere that you can hit a lob which he can't reach, what with the length of time that shot takes in flight.

The left-hander's slice to your backhand in the ad court is so advantageous a serve for him that he seldom tries to go down the center line. When he does, the ball will bounce into your body and cramp your swing, and once again you can only do your best with it, blocking or punching it low, and probably short, to either flank but more often down the line to his backhand. From this position, a lob to his backhand corner can also score a clean point on occasion.

I have said that my advice to a southpaw, playing a right-hander, would be to forget his "kicker" or twist service, and stick to his flat and particularly his slice. Almost all of them do. But what if your lefty opponent doesn't, and suddenly comes up with a "kicker?" Practically everything written above goes out the window, because the bounce will be in the other direction than all those previously discussed. So you may well ask how you can tell if a slice or a twist service is coming at you.

An excellent question.

The answer is that you *can* tell by the way the server tosses up the ball and by the direction of the swing of his racket. If he's serving a slice, he tosses the ball a bit away from his body and in front of it, and hits around and then through it almost exactly like a flat serve. But when he serves a "kicker," he throws the ball up directly over his head—almost a little backward—arches his back, and sweeps his racket up and over the ball and out from his body. It's a completely different sort of movement than the normal serve, and as you see it taking place you should realize instinctively what's coming. If you do, you have time to react. It's the same sort of reflex that you invariably have when you see your opponent chop or severely slice a ball rather than stroke it: you know the second he hits it that the ball will bounce short and low, and off to one side or the other depending upon whether he's right or left-handed.

Experience is the only way you can learn this sort of thing, but if you are reading a book of this type you are either already an experienced player or you soon intend to be. I can only offer one consolation if you are not. You're not going to see too many "kickers" when you're playing left-handers. Their slice serves are too effective for them to bother much about a more difficult serve.

Of course, there have been players who truly concealed what sort of serve they were delivering. It is said of Neale Fraser, the great Australian who won the U. S. Championship in 1959 and 1960 and the Wimbledon Championship in the latter year as well, that he tossed the ball exactly the same way no matter whether it was going to be flat, a slice, or a twist. Fraser and probably a few others possess this most unusual talent, but you can play tennis for a lifetime and never encounter one. It's not a worry to keep you awake nights.

All-court Stroking

All right. The ball has been served into court and returned by one or the other of you and is in play. What is there now to think about in particular when you're competing against a left-hander as opposed to your normal game against a right-hander?

Nothing very much—just the simple fact that every action of his is going to be the reverse of what you usually meet and that every action of yours ought to be keyed to meet that and to apply a diametrically different strategy of your own. As long as you bear that knowledge in mind every single instant during your match with a lefty, and are able to carry it out, you shouldn't have any more trouble with him than with a right-hander.

Do you begin to suspect that concentration really is a key factor in this game?

It may simplify your being able to picture what you're up against if you take your tennis racket and face a full-length mirror. Take a few tennis strokes while watching yourself in the mirror: try a practice service, a forehand, a backhand. Imagine that your mirror image is your opponent and that he's hitting the ball at you. If you have any tennis experience and instinct, it's very evident that this fellow is not your old friend and opponent, Mr. Right. You're facing a southpaw!

When right-hander meets right-hander, each one's forehand cross-court drive goes to the other's forehand, and each backhand cross-court to the other's backhand. Two solid and evenly matched players are likely to keep it up most of the day until one of them breaks the spell and whips a shot down the sideline. This changes things, at least for a moment, for now such a forehand shot goes to the other's backhand or vice versa. (Probably the return to that shot is another cross-court on the other diagonal and the players can pick up their exchange, only each is now consistently making the shots off his other wing. If it had started as a test of forehands, it changes to become one of backhands, and they may decide to keep that up the rest of the day. It can be very pretty for a while but it gets boring, both for players and spectators. Also, it isn't winning tennis unless one player is absolutely sure that he can out-steady the other at this sort of thing.)

When a right-hander plays a left-hander, this doesn't happen. Of course there can be long, cross-court ex-

Mirror tennis.

changes, but now one man will be hitting forehands every time and the other one backhands. Unless the latter possesses a remarkably strong backhand, he isn't going to allow this situation to continue to exist for too long, and the way he can change the pattern is once again to make a down-the-line shot. Now, if the cross-court exchange starts up once again the shoe will be on the other foot. Or, more accurately, the shots will be made from the other wing.

If that last paragraph sounds suspiciously like the one before it, you may not have distinguished the basic difference between the righty vs. righty match-up and the righty vs. lefty one. There *is* a difference, however, that should be appreciated:

Cross-court shots are hit much more frequently than down-the-line shots, because there's much more court into which to hit and so the margin of safety is much greater. If a right-hander is playing a right-hander, each is on equal terms in so far as the likelihood exists of one player taking an exchange of cross-courts off the same side as the other. But when a right-hander meets a left-hander, one or the other is likely to be at some disadvantage during a long cross-court exchange, since one will be pounding forehands and the other slicing comparatively defensive backhands. (If you have a backhand like Rod Laver's you are allowed to scream a protest at this point, but not if you're almost anyone else.)

Peculiarly enough for a left-handed man who developed probably the most powerful top-spin backhand drive in the history of tennis, Laver says in a chapter in the book *How to Play Tennis the Professional Way* that "most left-handers break down under pressure, especially on their backhands . . . his big, inherent weakness is his tendency to slice his backhand." Other authorities back up this thesis and the only explanation I've ever heard of why it may be so is that unthinking right-handed opponents are so accustomed to cross-courting their own backhands and confining their down-the-line shots to strokes they make off their forehands that lefties don't get too many backhands during play. As a result it doesn't become one of their strengths, whereas their forehands are likely to be particularly strong.

The comparatively weak backhand does seem to be true about most left-handers. It happens that it also is somewhat true of most right-handers! It's the rare exception who is as confident and powerful off the backhand as he is the forehand, be he right-handed or left-handed. The proof is that you often see a person "run around his backhand" to take the ball on his forehand, even in top-flight competition, but when did you last see anyone do the opposite?

So when you're playing against anyone, you're smart to try to exploit a weakness in his backhand, but this is particularly hard to do if you're competing against a lefty. Apart from your playing "mirror tennis," he has a trained stroke advantage on you that makes most of his strokes go automatically toward your backhand side. Most good lefties cross-court their forehand drives and undercut, or slice their backhands. Both of these shots go off to their right, which means they are directed toward your backhand. All a left-hander has to do to pound a right-hander's backhand consistently is to keep on doing what comes naturally. You, on the other hand, urgently need to concentrate right through the match on the fact that you are playing a left-hander, and that your instinctive tactics require reversal.

A word of consolation: this isn't *all* bad. When you're keyed up to concentrate steadily upon any one thing in a tennis game, you maintain your alertness about other factors. If you are an intelligent opponent, you are apt to be bearing down mentally throughout the contest more than he is, and this can turn the tide in your favor. If either of you becomes a little careless or sloppy, the odds are that it will be the southpaw.

And At the Risk of Repetition . . .

Everything else about handling yourself to best effect when playing a left-hander, once the ball is in play, involves nothing more than Variations on the Theme. It doesn't matter what shot you are attempting—it may be a drive, a slice or chop, a soft floater to the baseline, a drop shot or a lob—*in each case,* in addition to everything else you normally need to concentrate on, you should be thinking of making life as uncomfortable for the lefty as you can, and not be playing to his strength. This means, for most opponents, that the majority of your shots (not all of them, just the majority) should be directed to his backhand. Since this same philosophy applies when competing against the right-handers you usually encounter, your habits are ingrained and you instinctively, given a free choice, try to pass an opponent who has gained the net position with a drive to your right, or to his backhand. You must overcome that instinct when up against a lefty and, in the same alternative choice situation, hit out to your left.

Very few players can handle the more unusual shots as well off their backhands as they can from the forehand side. Specifically they are much less effective trying to return winners when you drop-shot them to their backhand side, or toss up a lob on that flank that they can reach for an attempted smash. On the whole—again not always because then a smart opponent will anticipate your every shot—go for the backhand side, and this means when you're matched against a lefty you always have to maintain that extra edge of concentration which tells you *which* side is his backhand. The answer, of course, is that it's the wrong one as far as your reflexes are concerned.

I have discoursed throughout as if it went without saying that everyone's backhand is a less effective shot than the forehand. That isn't exactly true. In many respects the backhand is a surer, easier stroke to make than the forehand and there are many instructors who teach it first to make that point with learners and get them over their instinctive distrust and lack of confidence in the stroke. I've been playing tennis with modest success for many years and I actually *trust* my backhand more than I do my forehand. It really never goes sour, and I don't need any warm-up to get the "feel," which is not true of my forehand. I seldom make an error off the backhand and I think I'm more accurate at "threading a needle" with it. The point is that very few players, including me, can hit a tennis ball as hard for a clean winner off their backhand as they can off their forehand, and that's what makes your opponent's backhand a good target to attack. He is not nearly as likely to blast you off the court with his return. If you are advancing to the net behind your shot, his backhand return is usually not going to have terrific pace on it which, if it's near you, means that you can put it away. If it's placed beyond your reach, at least you'll have a fighting chance to get to it before it passes you.

If you try a lob and don't make it deep enough, an opponent who is even a good weekend club player will smash it away for a winning point if he can take it comfortably on his forehand overhead. But among a crowd of weekend club players you can count on the fingers of one badly mutilated hand the number of them who can smash a backhand overhead. They are much more likely to meet the ball with a flick and send it back rather weakly, which puts you, the lobber who did not lob well but at least got the ball to the opponent's uncomfortable side, back again on the offensive.

Good Grief! If It's This Complicated Why Play Left-handers?

There are several good reasons. The first is that these days the woods, and the tennis courts, are full of them. Remember? Roughly one player in every six.

The second is that they are bona-fide, card-carrying members of the human race who are just as pleasant company, on and off the courts, as all those right-handers like you. If fate ordains that you will encounter a tennis player you should play him, regardless of race, color, or left-handedness. That's in the Constitution of the United States.

Most to the point, and seriously, is the third reason. One of the great charms of this most attractive of contestant games is its variety. You may compete more success-fully against an opponent who plays a baseline driving game, but how dull it would be if you never came up against a net-rusher or a chopper! You may have grown up playing on nothing but clay courts, but how wonder-ful all those new indoor courts are with their composition surfaces that permit you to play throughout the winter. It's a different game, but that's a challenge and the chal-lenge is a large part of the fun in tennis. Did you ever play on grass? It's a different game and you may be terri-ble, but it's a joy. Wind, and glaring sun, and fatigue are all challenges, but while you may curse them as you lose a point because of them, it's in the overcoming that the complete tennis player gains his greatest satisfaction.

Left-handed opponents constitute one of the most se-vere and interesting challenges in tennis.

To Sum Up

What edge does a left-hander have on you, and con-versely what edge might you have on him?

Physically, I can't believe there's any real distinction between you at all, other than you each eat and wield a tennis racket with different hands.

That fact is that the lefty has only one outstanding ad-vantage over you, but it has a variety of applications. He is accustomed to playing against right-handers and there's nothing even a little strange for him to be meet-ing still another one. You are accustomed to facing right-handers too, and now that you're bumping up against a southpaw you are forced to adapt your game. You have to concentrate all the way. This is true of all athletic face-to-face encounters—boxers and fencers, for example, probably have even greater problems against left-handed opponents than tennis players do. The closer the action, the shorter time in which to react to the unusual.

Certain specific difficulties that you, as a righty, have to face against a lefty have been pointed out, such as his ability to draw you wide out of court on your backhand when he serves a slice into your ad court. You might well query, "Well, haven't I the same advantage when I serve a comparable slice to his deuce court? Each of us can pull the other wide and force a difficult return. Each of us, in our respective opposite-court situation, can advance toward the net similarly, and each of us has to make equally sure that we cover the dangerous down-the-line return that this type of serve exposes us to."

All this is true enough. The difference which gives the lefty a big edge over you is not in theory but in practice. He is likely to set up this situation time and again, for he's constantly playing right-handers. You, on the contrary, have to reverse your normal ploys and use them on, and toward, the other side of the court than usual. You'll be attacking the receiver's backhand when you're serving from the right-hand court, and you ought to take up your position for the serve somewhat more to the right of center, perhaps even near to the corner. This is what you usually do when serving to a right-hander from the left-hand court: you move away from center to the left. Now that you're serving to a left-hander, however, it makes more sense in the ad court to serve from near the center line. That gives you a better chance to serve effectively down the center service line to his backhand or, if you serve wide to his forehand, you're in better court position to cover the down-the-line return.

There's little doubt that you are *able* to do these things, and all the other variations from what you're accustomed to do. The differences in stroke execution and technique are not enough to throw even a respectably good hacker off his game. The significant question is whether you *will*, for you may forget that you're playing mirror tennis and act instinctively.

That brings the whole affair in reality down to the matter of your ability to maintain constant concentration. That extra burden is your basic handicap, and if you can carry it effectively you'll be on even terms with a lefty who's of just about the same class as you are. Let your concentration flag, however, and as the match ends you'll be congratulating him on his victory. Your only consolation will be that he will have to be the one to jump over the net to extend his hand. His right hand, this time!

POSTSCRIPT TO CHAPTER 2

Although this book is concerned with how to play against, and with left-handed opponents and partners, a few words at the end of each instruction chapter about the basics of playing against or with anyone, be they left or right-handed, may be constructive. In focusing upon the very specific differences that exist when you find yourself on a tennis court with a left-hander, very little attention has or will be paid to the many fundamentals in tactics that apply against all rivals and with all doubles partners. No attempt will be made to write about grips and strokes and technique, but only a few reminders about strategy and tactics that fit into, and supplement those same aspects of the game that this book about left-handers attempts to supply.

The ultimate goal of all tennis instruction books is to teach you how to win. I yield to no one in my admiration for Grantland Rice's philosophy, so often quoted and beautifully printed and hung at major stadiums where players see it and walk out underneath it to the center court:

> *For when the One Great Scorer comes to*
> *write against your name—*
> *He marks—not that you won or lost*
> *—but how you played the game.*

I won't go into whether the age of commercialization has somewhat shaken this noble sentiment—I hope it hasn't—but as far as tennis instruction books are concerned the verse might well be parodied to be:

> *For when the One Great Scorer comes*
> *He writes not how 'twas done*
> *And if you played some flashy strokes*
> *But only if you won.*

When you step out onto a court to face a singles opponent whose game you don't already know, use the warm-up period to test possible weaknesses. Remember that the majority of points are won either on errors committed by the loser of the point or else on weak returns that the winner's shot has forced, leaving an easy putaway. Comparatively few points are won outright because of a blazing deep-court drive that's beyond the other person's racket. It looks good (if you keep it in court), it gratifies your ego, there will be occasions when you should attempt it, but on the whole, even if you make a fine stroke, a good player will be able to get to it and send it back. Meanwhile, if you drive it long or wide or catch the net, *you* will have made the error and lost the point.

Winning tennis is consistent tennis, whether you look good carrying it out or not. The best players look good, but not at the cost of not keeping the ball in play. Less sterling performers may not look so good but if they can keep returning the ball soundly, keeping their errors to an absolute minimum, they invariably beat a lot of much more stylish-looking and flashy opponents.

So in the warm-up session, probe your rival's strengths and weaknesses. If he seems to murder the ball on his forehand but pokes or slices a much weaker shot off his backhand (the usual case either with lefties or with righties), you know what to do. Playing a right-hander, direct most of your shots off to your right. Playing against a left-hander, change your normal instincts and aim for your left. If he's the exception whose backhand is stronger than his forehand, keep *that* in mind when you begin actual play. And remember that some tennis players perform better and hit their best shots when they have to go quite far to one side or the other, but are comparatively disconcerted by a ball hit right toward their bodies. This can be a most effective tip when you're serving to such a player.

When you're warming up, and your opponent is at net, see what sort of volley he seems to like to make off one side or the other and gear your thinking accordingly. Toss up some high balls ostensibly to give him a chance to practice smashes but really for you to see how he handles them. Does he smash down center? Does he angle them cutely toward the alley? Is he fundamentally not sure of his smash and merely sends the ball back, particularly on his backhand?

Try a couple of drop shots during the warm-up and see if he welcomes the opportunity to come up and take the net, and does it quickly and effectively. If he does, resolve to keep him away from the net as much as you can. Note how tall he is and how good a lobber you'll have to be to make that shot effective. See if he doesn't seem as happy hitting your soft deep shot or your chop as he does meeting fast pace.

Most players will show you that they thrive on one thing and don't like another nearly as well. The warm-up period may not be long enough for you to find out everything you'd like to know, but it's the place to start, and the first few games will either confirm or deny your findings. In either case remember Bill Tilden's famous maxim: "Never change a winning game. Always change a losing game."

All of these matters apply whether you're up against a left-hander or not. When you are, the thing that differentiates the situation is basically the requirement that if you're trying to exploit his backhand you do not hit off to your right, but rather to your left, and vice versa of course if he happens to be that rarity, a player with a stronger backhand than a forehand.

If you meet someone who's equally strong off both sides, and appears to have all the equipment to powder you to dust beneath his chariot's wheels, get out there and play your best. You might also pray your best: there's always the chance that he tires faster than you and if you can just keep the ball in play long enough to make it a lengthy match, he'll wilt. This is really more than the faintest of hopes: you can see it happen time and again, particularly at the club level.

CHAPTER 3

The Left-hander
as Doubles Opponent

A WINNING TIP

The moment you see that one of your opponents in a doubles match is left-handed, take note of which court he's going to receive service in, the right or the left court. Undoubtedly he'll be warming up on that side, so you won't have to ask him, which would be embarrassing, nor will you have to wait until the match is under way, when it's not too practical to stop and have a discussion with your own partner.

That discussion is what you two always ought to have, even if it's only a few words to confirm what each of you ought to know if you're regular partners. If the opposing left-hander is going to receive in his left-hand or ad court, both opponents are going to be able to take your wide serve and that of your partner on their respective forehands. They will be strong on shots to the outside, whether against service, cross-court drives, or when they're at the net. So play a team like this much more down the center of the court than you might otherwise. Three factors make this a good idea:

1) Each opponent will be taking center shots on his backhand.

Mine??? Yours??? CRASH!!!

2) They may be indecisive about which one should take a center shot. They may crash rackets, or bump into each other, or call "Mine!" or "Yours!" too late.

3) Playing down the center, one error factor is removed for your team. You won't hit out over the sidelines.

Some doubles teams with one righty and one lefty prefer to receive serve the other way around, with the lefty in the right or deuce court. Their theory is that a great deal of doubles play does take place down the center and they want to be particularly strong in that sector, with both men taking center shots on the forehand. Additionally, a pair that prefers this setup is probably a better-than-usual one, with each man confident that he is capable of returning a wide service cross-court to the server's feet: it is easier for a sound player to hit a backhand cross-court than down the line. If you encounter such a team (it's a comparative rarity), your discussion with your partner takes the reverse tack. Now you will try to serve wide most of the time to each court, get up to net, and try to put away the hopefully weaker backhand returns they must make. More of your volleys now will be directed to the outside, either sharply cross-court to the backhand side of the receiver's partner or, often an effective shot, right back toward the spot from which the return was hit by the receiver who, if you have served wide, will be scampering back to position and may well be caught "wrong-footed."

Shall we discuss what to do when you find you're playing a doubles team composed of *two* left-handers? No? Yes? Well, all right, but not for very long. For one thing there isn't too much to say except, as in the chapter about singles, everything you normally face becomes its mirror image. Instead of serving wide in the ad court and down the center line in the deuce court, you'll do the opposite. And so forth. The fact is that doubles play is usually at such closer quarters, without as much time for thought and execution as in singles, that you need all the concentration you can muster just to keep hitting well. It's almost asking too much for you to have the additional burden of remembering at every moment that both of your rivals are left-handed.

Forget it: it's not that critical. More to the point is the mathematical fact that if one in six players is left-handed, the odds against your meeting two of them on one doubles team are thirty-five-to-one against! If it happens, it happens. "Que Será, Será," as the lady is constantly singing. It isn't worth worrying about.

◎

Playing Against a Doubles Team,
One Member of Which Is a Lefty

Most of the general strategy you and your partner should try to bring to bear is embodied in "A Winning Tip" that leads off this chapter. What remains to be elaborated upon here are certain specific shots that fit into that pattern, plus a few other tactics you may find effective in such a match.

You already know what you and your partner should do *generally* when serving. (Once again, "generally" means on a majority of serves, not always! No good player lets his tactics fall into such a rut that his opponent doesn't have to be concerned about a change of pace and a mixture of shots.) On the whole, with your lefty rival receiving in the ad court, you'll serve more often down the center to both opponents. And in this circumstance, you and your partner should have one extra sharp arrow in your quiver, to be pulled out and used if either or both of you are not making out very well when serving to the lefty in the ad court. *Try seeing what happens if you adopt the tandem formation!* That seldom-used alignment seems almost to have been invented for this particular situation.

In the tandem or "Australian" formation, the man on your team who's serving (remember, we're talking only about service from and into the ad court) does so from as close to the center mark as he can. The net man, instead of taking up his customary position near the center of the right-hand box, aligns himself at net almost directly in front of the server: in other words he is just a

Tandem formation against a left-hander receiving in the ad court.

bit to the left of the center line. Neither man on your side has even his big toe in the right hand side of the court, and it's completely open, ready to be blasted by the lefty receiver's return of serve.

But is it? Geometrically, yes. In practice, however, this setup of yours may well present the most difficult problem for the left-handed receiver that he will have to face in the entire match. He has been conditioned through the years to returning just about every wide-angle serve cross-court. His control, and the dip he puts on a ball by virtue of the lefty's apparently inborn talent for topspin, makes that the ideal regular return of serve for him. It goes low toward the feet of the advancing server, and off to his backhand side. That shot is the basic reason why the southpaw is receiving in the left court, and his game is grooved so he makes it almost automatically. Additionally, on those occasions when the serve comes in to his backhand, a lefty invariably slices his return off along that same line, for the powerful backhand across his body is not his forte. (Yes, Rod Laver and Company, I know there are exceptions.)

So what happens if you throw the tandem combination at the left-hander who is receiving in the ad court? Both of his ingrained returns would take a line almost directly at the server's partner stationed at net. Bang, and away!

The lefty is forced to do something else, and he's uncomfortable doing it. The most natural response would be for him to try to hit down the line into the open court, but this is a return of service to which he seldom resorts. Also, unless he puts some zing into the shot and drives it close enough to the sideline to make it difficult for the server to reach in time, he won't be doing very much aggressively with his return of service. A short return into the open court, that has no real severity, lets the server move over to the right and up, take it on the bounce on his forehand, and close in to the net to join his partner. The result is likely to be that the lefty tries to go all out and make the brilliant winning sideline drive and, since this is both a hard shot under the best of circumstances, and an unnatural one for him in these particular circumstances, he's very likely to make an error and lose the point outright.

The lefty receiver's other alternative is to try to toss up a lob cross-court over the head of the opposing net man, stationed near center court. This, too, makes sense geometrically, since the server will probably be out of action on such a shot: he has to hustle over to his right to cover the open court. A perfect lob by the lefty here, particularly if he is capable of making one with topspin, to make it run after the bounce, is likely to be a winner. But how many of us, out of X-number of lob attempts, pull off perfect lobs? Additionally, in this particular circumstance, it's a most unusual shot for the lefty to try to accomplish. If no team has ever tried a tandem on him before, he would seldom or possibly never have tried it previously. The odds are better that he will either lob short enough so the net man can reach it, or that he will lob long and outside court, than they are that he will pull off the perfect lob that frustrates the tandem combination. If he does, hats off to him! See if he can do it again next time!

Don't ever allow opponents the chance to adopt to unusual conditions and so groove their reply strokes. If you try the tandem and it works, stick with it more or less as long as it continues to do so. If and when it doesn't, then go back to your normal pattern: you might well do so even earlier, despite your continuing to win points with the tandem, just for the sake of varying your game enough so that your opponents don't find answers by virtue of repetition.

If the lefty is receiving in the deuce court, you'll serve wide to both opponents, and once the ball is in play try to keep directing the ball toward the left-hander's alley when you can do it. You can employ this tactic as well when the left-handed opponent is serving. He has to be in the deuce court half the time. Take advantage of it.

When you and your partner are receiving serve, all players being more or less equal in talent, there's no doubt that you have something of a problem. For one thing, in doubles you only face the serve every second point during the game, and you haven't as much opportunity to tune your eye and reactions to a tough serve as you do receiving every point in a singles contest. That is true of every doubles game, but in this circumstance there is the added complication that on each of the games your opponents will serve, you will alternatively face a right-handed server for one game and then have to adjust yourself to a left-hander's delivery next time.

This is the aspect of facing a right-left team that calls most strongly for the characteristic that is so vital in playing singles against a lefty—*concentration*. The return of serve is all-important in any doubles match, and it is a very difficult thing to do both consistently and effectively when you have to alternate your thinking and your shots each time your rivals serve a game.

Once the ball is in play after the return of serve, doubles becomes a fast, close-in game with little opportunity for Deep Thinking. But the ball will never be in play unless you and your partner get those serves back in good style, and to do so you have to concentrate on which opponent is serving and what sort of spin he puts on the ball.

Consider what is likely to happen after one of your opponents serves, and remember that all the theory in this chapter's "A Winning Tip" applies only when *they* are receiving. When they have the serve, they'll obviously be switching courts on each point and hitting down the center, for example, isn't going to be the brightest of ideas when the left-hander is serving from the deuce side. Let's list the various situations that can exist:

1) *Left-handed Rival Serving from Deuce Court.* He serves and advances to net with the center and major portion of the court on his forehand. His right-handed partner is at net to the left, also with his forehand ready for any return his side of center.

The best return by whoever is making it on your team is probably a short, low, cross-court dink toward the on-rushing server's backhand. Alternatively he might try to pass the net man down the line, particularly if he's drawn wide out of court, or throw up a lob down that same line to the corner.

2) *Left-handed Rival Serving from Ad Court.* He serves a slice wide to your backhand or to your partner's, and comes in toward net. If you return a backhand drive, or slice, or dink sharply cross-court, he's likely to murder any one of them unless you angle it so well that it's out of his forehand reach. The percentages are all against your being able to pull that off, and you'll do much better if you direct your return closer to center court so that it reaches him on his backhand or, at worst, comes into or near his body so that he has to cramp a forehand shot. If he is a good server, this is the situation which is likely to test you most severely and your probable best bet is to hit a straight, or nearly straight shot

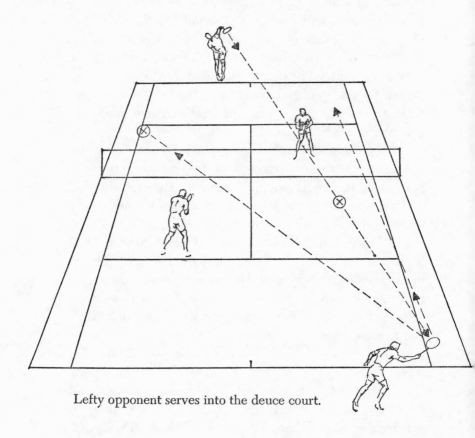

Lefty opponent serves into the deuce court.

down your side of the court. If you are drawn very far out of court you can try to pass the net man down his alley, despite that being on his forehand side. You need a favorable angle for that, however, as well as a brilliant forcing shot off your backhand, and in most circumstances you'll do better to drive or slice a shot near the center of the net, far enough away from the net man so that his attempt to volley it away off his backhand is im-

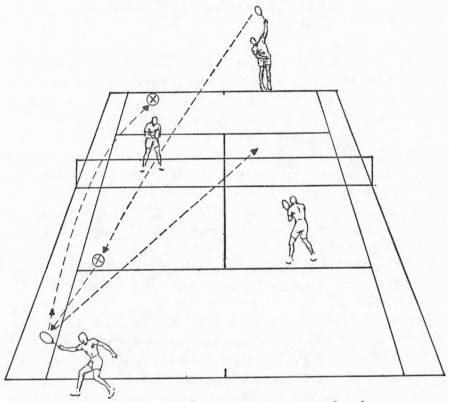

Lefty opponent serves into the ad court.

possible or extremely uncomfortable. Best of all, if you haven't that much confidence in your ability to pull off such a shot, hit a lob over the net man's head. It's the safest shot if the left-hander is giving you fits on his serve to this court. If you lob short, at least the net man has to retreat to mid-court to make his smash, and that gives you a chance. If you lob well to the baseline, either opponent who goes back to cover the lob is in trouble and you and your partner should both rush up and take the net yourselves, looking for a weak return that you can exploit.

3) *Right-handed Rival Serving from Deuce Court.* If he serves wide to you or your partner, the geometry seems the same in reverse as the above, but the situation is very different. You have a variety of choices, and any of them has a good chance of being the wise one. The ball approaches you on your forehand and while the same negative argument about the cross-court return might be raised here, you should be able to pound the ball hard enough, or accurately enough, to give the on-rushing server some trouble, even if he can take the ball on his forehand.

Alternatively, on this side you have the same possibilities of making a good return past, or over the net man. Finally, should the server put a ball down the center line onto your backhand, it is likely to offer you a very attractive opening between your two opponents and a straight or slightly cross-court backhand drive can be out of both of their reaches and go untouched.

4) *Right-handed Rival Serving from Ad Court.* Once again, this should be able to be handled. It's not as favorable a position as (3), but it's a lot better than (2). Unless the server has a very good "kicker" serve and uses it here, in which case you're in pretty much the same difficult position as in (2), you won't be drawn wide of court and you can respond with a cross-court dink, a passing shot if the angle is there, or a lob. All three, if you execute them well, take the ball to an opponent's backhand.

So your team's greatest challenge when receiving serve is to win a few points when your lefty rival is serving in

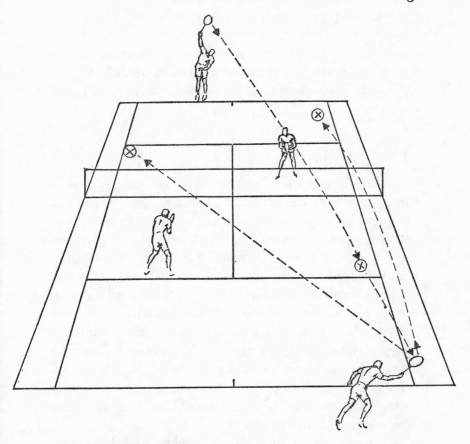

Right-handed opponent serving into the deuce court, left-handed one at net.

the ad court. It's always hard to break serve, but it's particularly so in this position, which has to take place at least twice when the lefty is at the service line, even in a love game. That is the prime reason why it's tough to break a southpaw serve in doubles, but be of good cheer. It's been done countless times before, and it will be again. Usually it's the result of hitting a forcing shot or a subtle one, like a dink, to one or the other's back-hand and moving in to try to take the net yourselves.

Then there's always the chance that the lefty will dou-ble-fault!

Your Opponents at Net

When your team is serving to rivals composed of a right-hander and a left-hander, each of them essentially stays on his respective side of the court when they come to net together. Depending upon which one plays on which side, you at least know throughout those games where your rivals' strengths and weaknesses are apt to exist. On most occasions the right-hander will be on your left as you face the net; the left-hander on your right. Their weakness should be down the middle. If they play the other way around, their strength should be down the middle and they may be susceptible to angled shots, but one way or the other you and your partner should know where you stand throughout your own serv-ice games, and act accordingly.

Now consider what takes place when they have serv-ice. When the right-hander is serving, you and your part-ner are facing a left-hander planted at the net, soon to be joined by a right-hander on the other side. Two games later the left-hander will be serving with his right-handed partner ready perhaps to poach, and the lefty will be coming up to join him. This means that you and your partner have to alternate your thinking about the best way to return service, and continue play, each time that

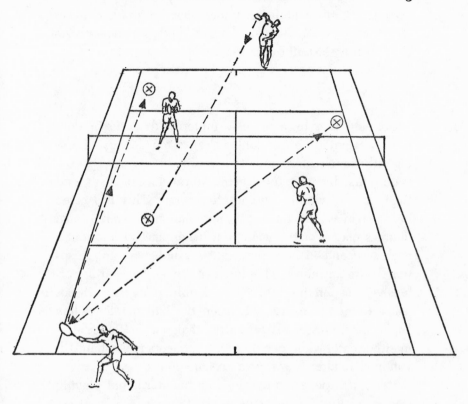

Right-handed opponent serving into the ad court, left-handed one at net.

you're on the receiving end. It takes a good deal of concentration and savvy to keep in mind that on *this* point it would be wise to drive down the center, whereas on the *last* point it wasn't. The burden is all on you and your partner: this is Strangeville for you. Meanwhile your opponents, well accustomed to each other's foibles, have no difficulty at all. They know what each other does in various situations, and they know what you're likely to do too, for you're just another right-handed pair such as they play against all the time.

The Lob

Lobbing is a tremendously underrated tactic in doubles. A talented pair of lobbers can often destroy an apparently much more talented doubles team with a Big Game, first by upsetting their natural flow of shots and then just by winning point after point. This has often been the case in top-notch national and international doubles play over the years, but it happens so frequently each weekend in club play that it's not even an exceptional circumstance. The lob can be a devastating offensive weapon for intelligent doubles players and not just a desperate measure to keep the ball in play when you're hard pressed. It's used for that too, of course, but in either case, when one of your opponents is left-handed, you have to alter the way you usually lob.

It was mentioned in the previous chapter about playing singles against a left-hander that you'd do well to steer your lobs off to your left so that, if they fall short, your opponent will have to smash off his backhand or, if they're good and deep, he'll have to make a backhand shot from the baseline. Lobbing is even more important in doubles than in singles, but now it isn't as easy as all that to remember each time what's best to do. On your service games your opponents will pretty well be in the fixed formation in which they started the point, probably with the right-hander playing on the deuce side and the left-hander on the ad side. So a center-court lob would be the best choice, not only forcing a backhand return from the opponent who takes it (unless he has time to run around it) but the delightful possibility that in a fit of excessive politeness each one will defer to the other and either let it drop between them or go for it too late. That doesn't happen often, but it does happen.

When you are receiving, the other team will be changing courts on each point. So on half of the points in such games, this same situation obtains. On the other half, lift your lob to either corner, preferably to the one occupied by the player with the weaker backhand.

If your opponents are of the school of thought that has the left-hander in the deuce court and the right-hander in the ad court, then you lob to the corners the majority of the time and only veer toward the center lob on those points when they're serving and their side-of-court formation is the reverse of how they started.

If you think this book is stressing the cerebral in tennis unduly, you have a point. There is no beating a player or a doubles team that can pound the ears off you, no matter how clever you are at theory. Certainly I would prefer to have a dumb Nastase (if there were such a thing) as my tennis doubles partner than I would Plato. All of us have been soundly thrashed at one time or another by opponents who appeared to play rather stupidly but were just too good for us, and no book advice is going to help much when that happens.

But *if* you're otherwise evenly matched against someone, using what Hercule Poirot refers to as "the little gray cells" can certainly swing the tide in your favor.

POSTSCRIPT TO CHAPTER 3

When you and your partner find yourself opposing a right-hander and left-hander pair you will, as pointed out at the beginning of this chapter, take particular cognizance of which is essentially going to play which court. Once that's determined and you have conditioned your minds to the set of circumstances that distinguish this match from the ones you usually play against two right-handers, use the warm-up session and the early games to see if either opponent, or both, show a weakness.

Almost all doubles combinations, whether they're two right-handers or one right-hander with a left-handed partner, have one man who is not as strong a player as the other. The difference between their respective abilities may be slight or it may be considerable. In either case, the initial strategy that you and your partner should bring to bear is to direct most of the traffic and pressure against the weaker player whenever possible. This not only may break him but it will often force the stronger player to overplay past his area of the court and leave what should be his responsibility open for your passing shot. The most frequent occasion on which this happens is when the weaker player is serving and his stronger partner, at net, has little faith in the server's ability to handle a good return with the force and bite that's required for him to get up to the net position himself. The stronger player decides that his team's best chance is for him to poach a lot, and this offers a counter opportunity for you and your partner to shift alternately from your basic plan, to pound the weaker player, and instead shoot passing shots down the alley behind the poacher.

If you're up against two slam-bang players who storm the net at every opportunity, lob them to death until they have to start backing up and then try to go up yourselves. If you are playing a team both of whom are essentially baseline strokers, get up to the net as much as you can, even on their serves, for they are doomed playing that way even if they are as good tennis players as you and your partner are. A good singles contestant, who is essentially a baseline player, can and often will beat a net rusher, but you have to advance to net in the doubles game. That's what winning doubles is all about.

When you're facing two right-handers, the man on your team who is playing in the deuce or right receiving side will be the one who most frequently answers a serve with a lob. He can lift it over the net man in front of him so that the ball lands near the left corner of the opponents' court, and this means the server has to hustle over there and make his return off his backhand. If you and your partner are by that time up at the net, as you should be, you have taken the offensive away from the serving team and are in excellent position to win the point.

The man in the ad or left court has nothing like the same good opportunity to use the lob effectively when you're facing two right-handers. His lob over the net man, if it's short, may be pounded away: his lob can be smashed from center to back court by the server on his forehand. It's like giving him another serve, probably from closer in, with the whole of your court available for him to choose his spot. That's why playing against a traditional right-handed team, you seldom see the left-court receiver lob.

Incidentally, the best lobs almost invariably are directed straight, parallel with the sidelines. There are occasions when a cross-court lob has to be employed but it's usually when you are in dire straits and need a time-consuming high shot to get back into position. It's a defensive stroke that has little chance of winning or helping you gain control of the point, because it invariably allows the opponent who's taking it to get to it in plenty of time.

However, when you are facing a right-hander paired with a left-hander, both you and your partner, no matter which court you play, have an extra good opportunity to lob effectively. When the right-handed opponent serves into the deuce court, your man there can do the same thing just as well as when a right-handed opponent is at net: the idea is still to drop that lob deep enough over the net man's head to give him a difficult overhead, or to force a backhand return from the right-handed server. When he moves over to serve from the ad court, your left-side receiver has the same constraint about *not* lobbing in that situation. So far there's no difference.

When the left-handed player serves from the deuce court, you as the receiver ought to forsake a lob return most of the time, for now the server can take it on his forehand. Besides, there are better things to do: a dink cross-court or a passing shot down the net opponent's alley.

Let us now consider when the left-handed player is serving from the ad or left side, *and remember that this is the way they are set up all the time when you and your partner are serving* if they receive with the lefty in the left court, as is usual. Now any shot down the middle is on both of their backhands, and "any shot" includes a lob. When you or your partner are receiving serve in the ad court, try lobbing down the middle. (Remember this is likely to be your toughest return anyhow, and the lob may well be your best way of handling it.) When you or your partner are serving, and have occasion to lob, again lob down the middle. In other words, more than half the time when you're playing a righty-lefty pair, the lob down the center court is a good idea. It has the additional advantage that your only concerns are height and depth. You need not worry about lobbing out over the sidelines.

The lob can be a great weapon in doubles, particularly in weekend class play, and the emphasis given to it here is more than justified.

CHAPTER 4

The Left-hander
as Doubles Partner

The winning tip that leads off this chapter has to do with trying to take advantage of the spin of racket at the beginning of the match, just as the tip did in the chapter about playing singles against a left-handed opponent. It also resembles that discussion in that the point involved has to do with where the sun is at certain times of day in relation to the server. In essence, therefore, this is the same tip, but it works out very differently in doubles than it does in singles, and you have to be aware of how to exploit it. The fact is that this doubles winning tip is sounder, can be used more frequently, and is a considerably solider ploy than the singles one. Never overlook trying to give your partnership an edge by thinking about it as the racket is spun, because if conditions are such that you are able to take advantage of it, it may well be worth many points in a set to you and your left-handed partner.

Playing outdoors at midday or within a couple of hours on either side of it, it's most likely that in one court or the other, whoever is serving will have to do so into the sun. Since teams change courts on the odd game, this works out to be fair enough to everyone—*if* everyone is right-handed. (Or if everyone happened to be left-handed, as a matter of fact, but this is of interest only to a mathematician. The odds against that happening, based upon our one left-hander in six players ratio, would be 1,295-to-1.)

But your partner is a lefty, and the blazing sun that bothers a server so much so frequently is almost always somewhat to the left or somewhat to the right of dead center looking down the length of the court. If it's off a bit to the left you, as a right-handed server, will toss your ball for service up and somewhat off to the right of your body, so you won't be bothered too much by the sun even if you're in the sun court. Alternatively, if the sun is off a bit to the right, where it might blind you on every toss, your left-handed partner would have no trouble at all if he were serving. His toss would be up and off to the left of his body.

Now remember that in doubles, *the same member of a doubles team always serves from the same side of the court*. This is the factor that is quite different from what happens in singles, and that is what makes this doubles ploy such a winner. You can set up a situation on days and at hours, when the sun is a tremendous handicap for the server facing it, so that neither you nor your southpaw partner will *ever* have the disadvantage! Obviously neither of you will have it in the shady court, so all you have to do is to make sure that the correct one of you—the one who tosses his serve *away* from wherever the sun happens to be—always serves in the sun court.

You may point out that this is all well and good but that the sun moves across the heavens (or at least it seems to) and that in a long match things may switch around so that you're then always at a disadvantage. Not true. By the time that the sun's position alters that much you will have played a set of tennis and after each set doubles teams do not have to maintain the order of service. Either one can start serving, when it's his team's turn, as a new set begins. So, if the position of the sun has altered, the other server on your team can take over the service on the sunny side of the court, even if he didn't do it during the previous set.

I repeat—keep this tip in mind at the outset of a doubles match such as has been defined and neither you nor your partner will ever be bothered on your respective service games by the blazing sun that may well be driving your opponents dizzy when they are serving. The idea that choice of courts may well be more advantageous to you than electing to serve first when competing against a left-hander in singles is an interesting one, but it's debatable. In doubles, if you have a left-handed partner and the sun conditions are clearly going to be a factor, I don't think there's any doubt at all that serving first is less advantageous than the natural edge of lefty-righty combination has as described above. At the spin of the racket you should try to maneuver things so that the stronger server of your combination serves your first service game, even if the other team serves first, but this may not be possible. Take my word for it or work it out for yourself— it may not be possible. If that turns out to be the case, let the weaker server start out. Setting up the situation so neither of you will ever be blinded by the sun is much more vital than the other consideration.

What are the details of how to work this out?

The best tactic you can adopt is to choose to serve if

you win the spin. If your opponents choose the court that enables your better server to serve first and for your team to preserve the advantageous setup you want, then you have the best of all possible worlds. If they choose the court that makes your weaker server serve first, let him.

If you lose the spin, your opponents will probably choose to serve first. Then you pick the court which, after the change-over that takes place after the first game, will allow your better server to start under the good setup you've predetermined. If for some mysterious reason your opponents win the spin and choose court, allowing you to serve first, let whichever player begin who is favored, or at least not handicapped, by the sun conditions, even if he is not the stronger server.

The first consideration in forming a partnership at tennis doubles with a left-hander is exactly the same as if you were teaming up with a right-handed player. Pick someone you like and who likes you. A tennis doubles pairing can no more survive its individual members criticizing and resenting each other than a marriage can. Apart from that, doubles is—or should be—a fun game. The pressures are less because they're shared. The rewards are more for partners who like and respect each other for the same reason.

Constructive ideas about tactics, or advice about strategy is one thing. But it's only welcome if you really know what you're talking about and your partner recognizes that fact. If one or the other of those points don't exist, silence is golden. What destroys more doubles teams than too overeager coaching by one member, however, is a show of anger or frustration when your partner misses a shot or fails to put away an easy kill. Sometimes this is actually and inexcusably expressed in words: more often by a scowl or a gesture of frustration. Everything will go from bad to worse if you treat a partner this way. It is a catastrophic way to act if you want to go on and win a match. Even more, it's deplorable manners and the first thing your partner should do after the match, whether you win or lose, is file papers for a divorce.

The second consideration when you've hooked up with a left-hander is to decide on which side of the court you'll each play when you are receiving service. There are two schools of thought about this subject and each has something to be said for it. Let's start with the one which probably is not valid for almost any doubles team whose playing talents are something less than superior —in other words, almost all pairs from rather good club or weekend players down the line to novices.

This school of thought maintains that since it's a basic tactic in doubles to hit down the middle of the court, you ought to put your strength there if you can. That means that the left-hander would receive in the right or deuce court, the right-hander in the left or ad court, so that any ball that comes down the middle can be taken by either on his forehand. The theory is that this is a greater advantage than the disadvantage that each now has to return a majority of serves off his backhand. That's a perfectly valid theory if you and your partner have extremely strong forehands, and particularly excellent forehand volleying at your disposal, and both of you are at least sound backhand players. If that's true, you are quality players and this may well be the formation that works best for you. There are many examples in national and international play where a doubles combination has teamed up this way with notable success, but you rarely see it at the club level and even at the star level it is not used by most partnerships where a lefty and righty are teamed.

So since books of this sort are not bought and studied by the Stan Smiths of this world, but by players like you and me, let's concede that there's something to be said for this argument and move over to the second, and infinitely preferable alternative for almost all doubles combinations (including Roy Emerson and Rod Laver).

That puts the right-hander in the right or deuce court, and the left-hander in the left or ad court. Instantly all becomes much more relaxing for you and me.

We will take most serves on our forehand: so will our left-handed partner. Since return of serve is so important in winning doubles, this is a tremendous edge. In particular, if he's a normal southpaw he'll be much more comfortable not having to return severe serves directed to his backhand. Similarly, you are in better shape having most serves going to your forehand as well.

Okay. Well and good as far as receiving serve is concerned, but what about that problem about most balls coming at you down the middle once the point is under way? Now you each have to take anything of that sort on your respective backhands. Is it all worthwhile? Should we have gone to the movies or tried to find an interesting orgy this afternoon instead of playing tennis?

Yes it is worthwhile. Either of your backhands may be quite up to handling center shots in the first place, and what you gain in other respects more than compensates for certain possible weaknesses here. Volleying off one's backhand is no harder than off the forehand: you are just not likely to be doing it with as much punch. But anyway, since the primary idea of the volley is to get the ball back deep and go to net for a kill hopefully on the ensuing return, in sacrificing power you may not have sacrificed all that much. Finally, if an easy return comes down the middle, it can be run around and taken on the forehand much more easily, and with much less disastrous consequences in pulling one out of position, than if you or your partner tried to do it on a soft alley shot.

So if you and your left-handed partner are of comparable ability, let him play the left court and you take the right. Definitely do that if he's better than you, but if he's considerably weaker than you, and his forehand is nothing that he's ever cared to write home to his mother about, it would probably be a good idea for you to take the left court yourself, just as you would do with a weaker right-handed partner. If one teammate is a distinctly stronger player than the other, a team is better off with him on that side; but unless the difference between your games is very apparent, stick to the left-hander on the left and right-hander on the right formation.

Keep in mind that when your southpaw partner is serving in the ad court, his intense slice is going to pull the opponent who is receiving further out toward the sideline than usual. So tend to edge over a bit more toward the alley than you normally might, or you may be exposed to a very makable passing shot down your alley by the receiver.

Conversely, when your left-handed partner is serving

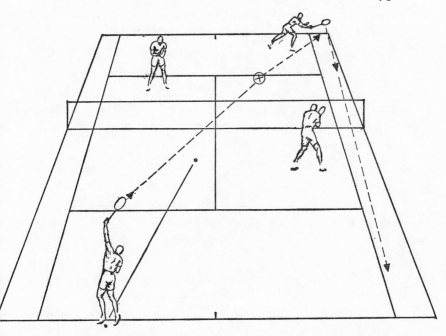

Your left-handed partner serving from the ad court.

in the deuce court, that is not going to happen on a slice and you may be more prone to take a chance now and then and poach when you see the serve coming in directly to the receiver, or to his backhand. Any time you poach you expose yourself to the passing shot down your alley, so you can't overlook that dangerous possibility. On the other hand, the percentage is much less that this shot will be attempted by the right-court receiver, because a good left-hander's serve to him in that box offers a poor angle. He is much more likely to return the service cross-court, very possibly with a dink shot, and if he doesn't execute it perfectly a dink travels slowly enough

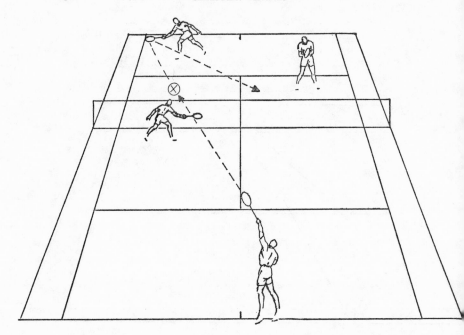

Your left-handed partner serving from the deuce court.

that, if you're poaching, you have a good chance to reach it and put it away with your forehand.

When you yourself are serving, and your lefty partner is at the net position, remember that your team has something of a disadvantage when you're serving from the right-hand court because all returns down the center will be on the backhands of both you and your partner. Your slice serve will go wide to the receiver and open the likelihood of an attempt by him to shoot one down your partner's alley, so in this position it's usually best for your partner to hold his ground, protect the alley (which is

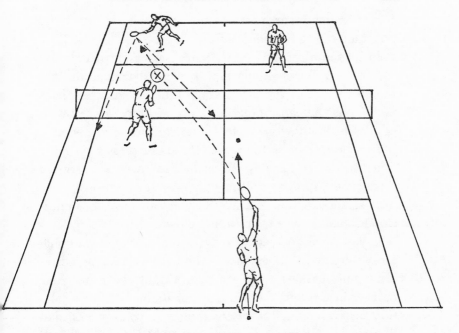

You serve from the deuce court and your left-handed partner is at net.

on his forehand), and only try to cut off a return on his other side if it's clearly within his reach and tempting. You are in a better position to take the majority of the shots down the center on your backhand, either on a center-court volley or on the bounce and, of course, you're responsible for a sharp cross-court drive or dink to your forehand.

When you are serving from the left or ad court, that's the situation for your partner to do most of his poaching. Your slice serve will not be very wide, since it slides off to your left, and this is likely to encourage a cross-court return which your partner may be able to reach by poaching on his forehand side.

In all these cases, if either you or your partner decide to vary serve by changing to a "kicker," make certain that the server warns his net partner that it's going to happen so that he can protect his alley. Nothing leaves more egg on a doubles team's face than to have the net man solidly passed while the server stands helplessly near the other corner, or in mid-court if he's followed his serve in toward net. You can do this either by surreptitiously saying "kicker" to your partner, or you can have an understood signal between you to that effect.

If you have decided to play in the more conventional formation, and the one that is the better for most righty-lefty combinations, with you in the right court and your partner in the left, there is one not unimportant consolation for you about the disadvantage of your team's likelihood of being weak down the center. It's true that each of you will be taking center shots on your respective backhands but there's one situation that's not infrequent when this is not bad. It does assume your frame of mind is adjusted to the probability and you train yourself to handle a ball the right way when the situation comes up.

In doubles, the whole idea is for both of you to get up to the net, side by side. A number of shots will inevitably come directly *at* you or your partner, rather than off to one side. Whether you're a righty or a lefty, the best way to handle a drive directly into your body when you're at net is to take it with a backhand volley. You can see the sense in this readily. If you attempt to take such a shot with a forehand, you have no arm room at all: your arm must cross in front of your body and no matter how far (and clumsily) you do this, the racket going back off in the other direction has to be cramped tightly against you with your wrist bent to its limit. On the other hand, if you volley a direct shot to your body with your backhand, your arm can be extended naturally away from your body and your bent elbow and firm wrist bring the racket back in front of you for a proper backhand volley.

These facts, of course, are equally true for two right-handed partners. The aspect that gives them particular significance for a right-hander left-hander combination is that so frequently they know that it's likely one or the other is going to have to return center shots off the backhand and, if they are smart, they practice it and are alert for it in actual play. Two right-handed partners, who have no such concern all the time, are not particularly alert to it. This does mean that on shots into one's body at net, the righty-lefty pair should have some slight edge, even if a major portion of it is only mental preparation.

But the basic advantage you have when you're partnered with a left-hander as a doubles team is much like the one the southpaw singles player has when meeting a right-hander. It's the same in that your opponents have to face something they don't usually encounter, and they have to alter and accommodate their natural strokes and instincts.

Additionally, when two right-handers play against a doubles team like yours, it is probably even a more upsetting task than for a right-handed singles player meeting a lefty opponent. At least in that case the singles

The wrong way to handle a ball hit directly at you.

The right way to handle a ball hit directly at you.

player can concentrate on *always* doing the opposite of what his normal procedure and tactics would be.

A right-handed doubles team, however, is faced with a whole series of constantly shifting situations when it's up against a pair composed of a right-hander and a left-hander.

They may both be at net, and if they've been receiving serve they will each be protecting their respective alleys off the forehand. They may then be exposed to a good center court attack, *but*

They may have crossed, as the result of a lob or some other circumstance, and now they're particularly strong down the center, *and*

When they are serving, they are sure to be first in one setup, and then in the other, on alternate points. It's a great deal to try to remember and to adjust to when that poor pair of right-handers may have all they can do just to make good strokes and keep the ball going over the net.

Meanwhile you and your left-handed partner have no such concerns at all, since each of you is accustomed to play against right-handers. You can concentrate on the normal business at hand, play your regular game, and focus your mind on such fundamentals as keeping your eye on the ball, preparing your racket properly on the backswing, turning your body to the net, getting down for your volleys, and hitting out on your shot with top spin and follow through. Easy.

Do you receive the impression in this chapter that I think you're in luck and that you have something extra going for you, all other things being equal, if you are paired with a left-hander in doubles?

You're right. I do.

POSTSCRIPT TO CHAPTER 4

The subtle working partnership that any successful doubles team develops has at least as much to do with their success as individual talents have. Down through tennis history there have been a great number of cases where two of the best singles players in the world have linked up to form a doubles team and nothing very startling resulted. Conversely, every now and then a doubles team emerges from the partnership of two good, but not outstanding players, which sweeps everything clean that it encounters. The Kinsey brothers, neither of them really a top-ranking singles player, was a notable example of a world-famous doubles team in the earlier part of this century. What is more, certain individuals have a specific talent for doubles play. Probably the two men of our time who are famous as having been able to team up with any star and produce a great doubles team were George Lott of America, and John Bromwich of Australia. Neither of them ever scaled the absolute summit of international play in singles, but each teamed with a variety of partners to form a number of the best doubles teams in the world during their time. Similarly, when France dominated the tennis world in the late 1920s with their "Four Musketeers," three of them, Lacoste, Cochet, and Borotra were among the world's best at singles. The fourth Musketeer, Jacques Brugnon, never made a dent in international play at singles, but he was the man who could team with any of the other three to make an unbeatable team. Today, Bob Lutz and Owen Davidson are good examples of such players.

So partnership, understanding, and empathy are tremendous factors in molding the effective doubles combination, and fairly inevitably the player who has a particular feeling or genius for the game of doubles, like Lott or Bromwich or Brugnon, is its guiding spirit, even though the other player may be the big performer who puts away most of the smashes and inspires the greatest applause from the gallery.

The spiritual leader of a doubles team, if such a term can be used without blushing, encourages his partner while performing his own role. He never nags or browbeats. He applauds good shots by his teammate and completely disregards bad ones. It's impossible to try to give your partner lessons while you're playing. Either you wait until you're having a cool drink together later, or maybe you never bring up the subject of your partner's derelictions at all.

Do bear in mind that a discussion of team tactics and strategy is not only admirable but recommended. That's a mutual affair, even if you're the directing Brain, and it doesn't denigrate your partner's performance. But as far as strokes are concerned, accept the partner you have for what he can do, or else go looking for another. If he needs tips on his volley, he'll be better off consulting the local professional than he will be listening to you.

The spirit that must be engendered in an effective doubles team is confidence in each other. After a team has been playing together for some time, reactions become instinctive and it's seldom that anything need be said or signaled to tell the other player anything. Of course, the player at whom the ball isn't coming can often have a better instinct that a close ball will be out, and he should call "Leave it!" to his partner. Similarly there will be occasions when the standard pattern of your team play will be upset by an opponent's shot, and while the unnatural man to make the return dashes to run down the ball, he may call "Cross!" to his partner to indicate that he can't get back into position on his side of the court.

There will be times when it's questionable who should take a ball, and this is likely to be particularly true when you're partnered with a lefty and he is stationed in the left court. Your opponents, if they're smart, will direct lots of balls down center court into the area which is on both of your backhands. It is infinitely preferable for the one who thinks he can handle the ball better to call "Mine!" than for the man who is doubtful to call "Yours!" It's the virtue of Positive Thinking.

If neither of you call for the ball on a questionable shot, the chances are that the one who made the last return should take this one too. He's in the flow of play on this point and he's more likely to see the angle and maintain the pitch than the other player intruding from a comparatively flat-footed start.

The traditional way of taking up your respective positions when your team is serving is best most of the time, and it's not suggested that you vary it as long as things are going well. But suppose your left-handed partner is having trouble holding his service games, and even has lost one or two of them. Remember that he is most effective when he's serving his slice from the ad court: probably he's losing when he's serving from the right. You might well try the "Australian" position in this situation, and see if you can do any better. ("Change a losing

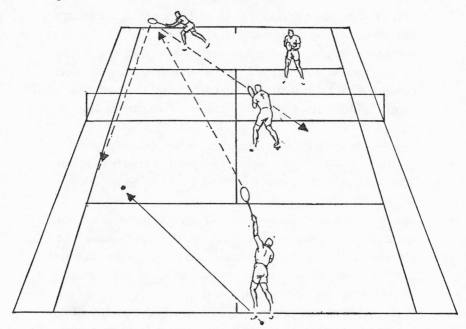

The tandem formation may be effective when your left-handed partner is serving from the deuce court, if he is having trouble holding service. If *you* are having similar trouble, try the tandem from the *ad* court when you are serving. You can see how this would look by holding this drawing up to a mirror.

game"—remember?) Your lefty will serve from the right court, but standing nearer the center marker. You will take your position at net in the right court too, ready to cut off the cross-court drive or dink that's been frustrating your team.

If the receiver hits one toward you, you should be able to handle it readily. Your opponent recognizes this and will almost surely send his return down the line, but two things may make this work out well for you. The first is that it isn't his natural return of serve in this court and he may make an error to lose the point immediately. The second is that your team isn't really exposed to the shot: serving from near center your left-handed serving partner will immediately cut for that side after delivering his serve, and will be over there in plenty of time to handle the return of serve on his forehand. The "Australian" formation is not as sound fundamentally as the conventional one, but it can be mighty effective if used at the proper spots, particularly to change the way things have been going for you if they haven't been going well.

It's a truism in weekend play that too often doubles teams go through a point with one man up at the net and the other in the backcourt. There are many rational explanations for this. If the rear-court man is the server or the receiver, he may not feel that his mid-court volley is good enough for him to advance. He may be lazy, or fat and forty. Fair enough. But any respectable player can at least generally come in on the second shot he has to make, taking it on the bounce from a position somewhat closer to the net. That is the least he can do, and that is what he must do on most points. Doubles matches are won at the net, and doubles partners should be aligned side by side. This is true both of men's and women's doubles: an exception can sometimes be made in that delightful game called mixed doubles, where the front-back formation often is the best idea. Mixed doubles is a very separate game, calling for different strategies, and it's a proper subject for another whole book of this type. That is one reason why no more than this passing reference is indicated, but there is still another reason.

Much of what is written in *Sinister Tennis* does not apply to most mixed doubles matches. For one thing, short of players of national-ranking caliber, most women tennis players—very good ones too, at the club level—thrive on hitting flat drives and do not rely upon spin much, or at all. This is not only true of how they stroke during court play but also of their serves. You seldom see a woman, who isn't a top tournament contestant, slice her service severely and you practically never see one deliver a "kicker." Therefore most of the aspects in this book that relate to the unaccustomed spin of the ball, when hit by a left-hander, don't pertain because the ball usually takes its normal bounce.

Women hit a tennis ball just as squarely, solidly, gracefully, and well as men of comparable abilities but, on the whole, they are not as powerful. A man who is no better a tennis player than his woman partner is a much more dangerous smasher of an overhead, for example, simply because he's stronger. This factor is so important in mixed doubles, a game where the lob is employed as a weapon more than in any other tennis encounter, that it overrides other considerations. So if you are a right-handed man, paired with a left-handed woman partner (who isn't a *much* better player than you are), it's almost invariably the better idea for you to play in the ad, or left side of the court, even though that's contrary to the conventional alignment. The disadvantage is that each of you will have to receive a lot of your opponents' serves on your respective backhands, but the advantage of your being in the better position to handle lobs, and the subsidiary one that you'll both be stronger on center court shots, outweighs that.

If you are a right-handed woman, teamed with a left-handed man, all is well. You will play the right court and he the left, just as a righty-lefty men's or women's doubles team would probably choose to station themselves.

It has been said more than once that doubles matches are won at net. But they won't be won unless, once you or your partner are at net and get a return you can reach, you haul off and put the ball away. If you can smash it anywhere in court so that no one can return it, fine. If you can angle it sharply off so that no one can reach it, fine. But win or lose the point right there. Don't temporize. If you just execute an in-between, don't-take-a-chance shot, you've not only lost all your advantage but probably have made yourselves sitting ducks for your opponent's next shot. Nothing is easier than to cream a pair at net after a weak, center-of-court return from one of them.

Most tennis players enjoy singles when they're young and think of doubles as a pleasant but definitely subsidiary game. They like having the burden completely on themselves and they revel in the undoubtedly greater physical action that singles offers. Usually they start their tennis careers by concentrating on baseline play and only advance to the net when they're drawn there, or when they've made a particularly effective forcing shot. Then it would be insane not to seize the advantage and crowd the opponent.

But if you are born with the instincts of a George Lott or a John Bromwich or a Jacques Brugnon, you may well like doubles better right from the start. Almost unquestionably as you grow older, and either your common sense or your doctor tells you to turn more to doubles, you'll be doing so. When that happens, no matter how loyal your old feelings may be that singles is *the* game of tennis, the chances are that you'll find doubles more fun. It's a game with many more complexities—a game that is won with the head as much as with the hand. Although it is certainly not as strenuous and demanding of physical condition, the action in first-class doubles is infinitely faster than in singles. If you have a compatible partner —and find another if you don't—you share both triumphs and disasters. The one is sweeter for the sharing, the other more consoling.

Doubles is a great game and if you, a right-hander, are lucky enough to have a good left-handed partner, you can make it a great winning game.

With the co-operation of the United States Lawn Tennis Association, Doubleday has published the following titles in this series:

SPEED, STRENGTH, AND STAMINA: Conditioning for Tennis, by Connie Haynes with Eve Kraft and John Conroy.
Detailed descriptions of exercises for tennis players, and suggestions for keeping in shape.

TACTICS IN WOMEN'S SINGLES, DOUBLES, AND MIXED DOUBLES, by Rex Lardner.
A book for women tennis players, with specific suggestions for taking advantage of opponents' weaknesses.

SINISTER TENNIS, by Peter Schwed.
How to play against left-handers and with left-handers as doubles partners.

The following titles are in preparation:
FINDING AND EXPLOITING YOUR OPPONENT'S WEAKNESSES
RETURN OF SERVICE
COVERING THE COURT
GROUND STROKES
SPECIALIZATION IN SINGLES, DOUBLES, AND MIXED DOUBLES
THE SERVE AND THE OVERHEAD
THE HALF VOLLEY AND THE VOLLEY
TEACHING TENNIS
TENNIS AS A THERAPY
SKILLS AND DRILLS

Each book in this series is illustrated with line drawings and is available in both hardcover and paperback editions.

Q